TROLLEYBUS MEMORIES
BRIGHTON

Glyn Kraemer-Johnson
and John Bishop

First published 2007

ISBN (10) 0 7110 3199 1
ISBN (13) 978 0 7110 3199 9

© Ian Allan Publishing 2007

Published by Ian Allan Publishing

an imprint of Ian Allan Publishing Ltd, Hersham, Surrey, KT12 4RG
Printed in England by Ian Allan Printing Ltd, Hersham, Surrey, KT12 4RG

Code: 0709/B

Visit the Ian Allan Publishing website at www.ianallanpublishing.com

Narrative by Glyn Kraemer-Johnson
Photographs selected and captioned by John Bishop

Contents

Front cover: AEC-built No 27 of 1939 heads down Beaconsfield Villas on its way back from Hollingbury in May 1961. *John Bishop / Online Transport Archive*

Back cover: This view of 1939-built AEC / Weymann No 25 under the Larkfield Way turning circle in May 1961 shows just how attractive were Brighton's trolleybuses, both in terms of design and livery application. *John Bishop / Online Transport Archive*

Title page: Displaying just a route number, No 34 is pictured at Fiveways in the early 1960s, having just emerged from Preston Drove on the left. *Malcolm Keeping*

This page: This busy scene at the Old Steine c1960 shows No 34, again with just the route number displayed. By this time the wiring for routes 41 and 42 had been removed; one of the AEC Regent IIIs that replaced trolleybuses on these routes is standing in the background by J. Lyons. *W. J. Haynes / Southdown Enthusiasts' Club*

Introduction

The first time I saw one I didn't like it. It wasn't right.

Born in Dartford, I'd spent the first five years of my life riding on London Transport Leyland trolleybuses on route 696 when visiting my grandparents in Bexleyheath. These huge six-wheeled monsters would glide silently around Dartford Market Place, climb effortlessly up West Hill and then cruise along the main road to Crayford and on to Bexleyheath and Woolwich. In terms of body design, livery, destination screens and interior décor they were totally different from contemporary London motor buses, and, just in case you were in any doubt, each carried an LT roundel proclaiming that this was a 'Trolleybus'. To a four-year-old the walk from the rear platform to the much-coveted front seat seemed like a marathon!

Then, in 1946, my family moved to Brighton, and I came face to face with my first Brighton Corporation trolleybus. As I said at the beginning, they weren't right. They had an axle missing, sporting a mere four wheels, and, apart from lacking a bonnet and radiator, looked more-or-less the same as many of the motor buses operating alongside them. I treated them with disdain. In any case, I lived in Hove and went to school in Kemp Town, so I had no cause to use them.

I had, however, become familiar with their siblings, the 21 AEC Regent motor buses delivered at the same time in 1939 and carrying virtually identical bodies by Weymann. Although I was beginning to form what was to be a life-long love of Bristols, these Regents evoked memories of London Transport, their 8.8-litre engines being very 'LT' (well, 10T10 actually), and whenever I rode on one I greatly enjoyed the experience.

Then we moved to Lewes Road, served at that time by routes 48 (trolleybuses), and 38 (Corporation Regents), as well as Southdown's services to Coldean and Moulsecoomb (utility Guys) and its country services to Lewes and beyond (mainly prewar Leyland TDs). At that time Southdown operated 'protective' fares to discourage short-distance passengers, so it was usually by trolleybus or Regent that I travelled. Shortly afterwards I gained a place at Varndean Grammar School, conveniently situated on the 46 trolleybus route.

My first girlfriend lived in Hollingbury on the 26 route, so, as car ownership by teenagers was virtually unheard of at that time, whenever I took her out it was by trolleybus, and having taken her home I would return to the town centre at high speed on the last 26.

By this time my early scorn of these vehicles had turned into a strong affection. I had come to know the Brighton trolleys intimately, and although they weren't perhaps as individual as the motor buses they certainly had their own characteristics.

In 1961 I got married, and the Brighton trolleybus system closed. I'm not sure which was the greater loss — my freedom or the trolleybus! It was a very sad time, especially when I saw what replaced them!

Although the text is arranged chronologically, this book is not intended to be a detailed history; that has already been done by those more qualified to describe the technicalities of the system. No; this is more a collection of memories and anecdotes from those who lived with and loved the Brighton trolleys. Both authors spent their formative years in the town, my own experiences being mainly as a passenger as well as an enthusiast. John is well known for his knowledge of the trolleybus and for his travels worldwide, filming and photographing the species. It was the Brighton system that spawned and nurtured his interest.

The Brighton trolleybus system lasted 22 years, and at the time of writing it is 45 years since its closure. Nevertheless, we have managed to find a former trolleybus driver who has provided us with some of his memories from the other side of the front bulkhead.

A fine collection of photographs has been gathered together from various sources, including many from John's own camera, most of which are previously unpublished. Cuttings from the local press are also included, all of which we hope has gone to create a publication that will evoke fond memories for those who knew the system and will provide a lighthearted insight into trolleybus operation in Brighton for those too young to remember them.

In conclusion we would like to thank Andrew Henbest, Malcolm Keeping and Pat 'Paddy' Slattery MBE for their not inconsiderable help in producing this book.

Glyn Kraemer-Johnson
Hailsham, East Sussex
June 2007

Right: A tranquil scene at Hollingbury in the latter years of the system with No 44 waiting to depart on the 26 to the Aquarium and No 27 similarly going to the Aquarium but by the 46 route via London Road. The conductor stands by No 27 underneath the overhead that embodied facilities to turn completely. It has to be said the overhead was a credit to the Corporation which maintained the whole system. *Malcolm Keeping*

1. Background

Electric traction proper came to the streets of Brighton in 1901, when Brighton Corporation opened its tramway system using four-wheel open-top cars, a configuration that was to remain the standard until the system closed in 1939. Hitherto transport in Brighton and Hove had been provided by the Brighton, Hove & Preston United Omnibus Co, which had made forays into electric propulsion with a number of second-hand battery-powered 'Electrobuses' that did not prove particularly successful. Later Tilling-Stevens petrol-electric vehicles were tried, and, whilst these proved more efficient, they did not offer the smooth riding qualities

offered by the recently introduced 'trackless trolleys' as they were known.

Its interest in electric traction prompted the BH&PUOC to apply to Parliament for powers to operate trolleybuses within the two boroughs as early as 1911. These powers were never used, however, and the following year both Brighton and Hove corporations made similar applications to operate trolleybuses within their respective boroughs. As a result two 'trackless trolleys' were hired to demonstrate their qualities to the two municipalities.

First came what was termed a 'Railless Car' built by the RET Construction Co, which operated during December and

January 1913/14. A short length of wiring was erected along Brighton's London Road on which the bus was demonstrated. Of open-top, open-staircase design, the vehicle used the conventional method of current collection, with twin spring-loaded booms holding the trolley head against the underside of the wires.

Eight months later, in September 1914, a similar experiment took place in Hove, wiring being erected from Hove station along Goldstone Villas and George Street. Again the blue-and-cream bus was of open-top, open-staircase configuration and was borrowed from Keighley Corporation. This vehicle, however, used the

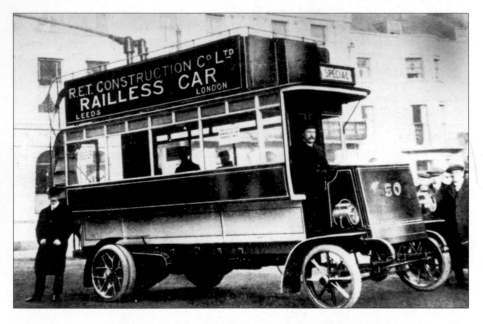

Left: Regrettably very few photographs exist of the first trolleybus to operate (albeit experimentally) in Brighton. The vehicle in question, built by the RET Construction Co, was used on demonstration between December 1913 and January 1914 on a short stretch of London Road just north of St Peter's Church. *Mervyn Stedman collection*

Left: The experimental RET demonstrates the manœuvrability of the trolleybus over the tram by passing a horse and cart in London Road; the outstretched trolley booms are shown to good advantage. It would nevertheless be another quarter century before trolleybuses replaced Brighton's 3ft 6in-gauge tram system. *Mervyn Stedman collection*

Cedes Stoll method of current collection whereby a four-wheel trolley ran along the top of the wires, being towed by a cable attached to the bus.

Both demonstrations proved successful, but in spite of this no other trolleybus ever operated in Hove, and it was to be more than 20 years before another ran in Brighton.

The next development took place in the mid-'Thirties, when Brighton Corporation again decided to apply for powers to operate trolleybuses. This resulted in the Brighton Corporation Transport Act (1938), which allowed for the Corporation's trams to be replaced and for all bus services operated by the Corporation and the Brighton, Hove & District Omnibus Co Ltd (as successor to Thomas Tilling) to be co-ordinated, with revenue and mileage being shared on a 27.5% / 72.5% basis in favour of BH&D.

Prior to reaching its decision the Corporation had had further vehicles on loan for demonstration. First, at the end of 1935, had been Portsmouth Corporation No 20 (RV 6378), a Cravens-bodied AEC 961T, which was operated on a stretch of wiring erected along Union Road, to the north of The Level. The same stretch of wiring was used in January 1936 when London Transport AEC No 61 (AHX 801) was put through its paces. Like most of London's trolleybuses it was built on a six-wheel chassis. Brighton, however, opted for the shorter four-wheel version, and AHX 801 was destined to be the only six-wheeler ever to operate in the town.

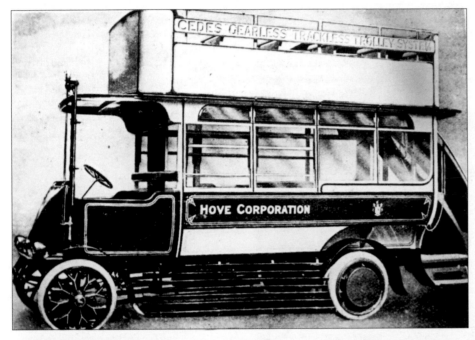

Left: There has always been a certain rivalry between Brighton and Hove, and in 1914 Hove Corporation, which never favoured the tram, had its own stretch of trolleybus wiring erected between Hove station and the bottom of George Street. The system employed the Cedes-Stoll principle, whereby an over-running trolley ran on two wires suspended overhead; the device attached to the nearside front of the vehicle conducted the electric current to the drivetrain. *Mervyn Stedman collection*

Above: A posed view of the vehicle demonstrated to Hove, showing how well presented the vehicle was, complete with Hove Corporation fleetname and coat of arms and the proud proclamation: 'CEDES "GEARLESS" TRACKLESS TROLLEY SYSTEM'. The photograph dates from August 1914, by which time the country was at war with Germany, one of the countries responsible for the Cedes-Stoll system and chassis manufacturer. This would prove the main stumbling-block for any orders, although great play was made at the time of the fact that the Dodson body, along with some of the electrical equipment, was British. This scene in Goldstone Villas, Hove, shows just how much interest was generated by the vehicle. Interestingly one can see the large rear wheel hub, where the electric motor was located — a feature adopted in more recent times by German manufacturer Neoplan for its trolleybuses. *Mervyn Stedman collection*

Left: This final view of the Cedes-Stoll trolleybus in Goldstone Villas shows the current-collection cables leading up to the overhead wires. On the top is the trolley, which would be drawn along behind the vehicle or, when descending a hill, would roll ahead, being stabilised by the heavy weight seen here hanging above the upper-deck passengers; the stretch of overhead wiring erected in Hove included a tram-style crossover with a small gap for the weight to pass through. The system was not adopted in Hove, and the trolleybus duly headed north to Keighley, Yorkshire, where a lengthy system was in operation. A similar system of current collection, albeit with one cable, remains in use to this day near Berlin, powering an electric motor on a ferry. *Mervyn Stedman collection*

Left: Late in 1935 a section of trolleybus wiring was erected in Brighton alongside The Level in Union Road, not too far from the original installation of 1913, and this was used to demonstrate Portsmouth Corporation English Electric-bodied AEC trolleybus No 20 (RV 6378). As apparent from this photograph, taken on 12 December, the vehicle generated a great deal of interest — so much so that Brighton Corporation decided on the AEC chassis for its order for delivery in 1939. *Brighton & Hove Herald*

Above: In 1936 the same stretch of wiring was used to demonstrate a six-wheel trolleybus. In less-than-clement weather conditions London Transport AEC No 61 (AHX 801) stands on the north side of The Level as Class E tram No 69 looks on disapprovingly. This would prove to be the only three-axle trolleybus ever to operate in Brighton. *A. D. Packer collection*

Above: An offside view of the Portsmouth Corporation AEC, again showing the degree of interest locally in the proposal to replace the trams. The flat caps and the number of pedal cycles are indicative of how much life has changed over the past 70 years. *Brighton & Hove Herald*

2. The Trolleybuses

Following the initial experiments Brighton Corporation decided to order 44 AEC 661T four-wheel chassis, on which were mounted 54-seat Weymann bodies. Twenty-one AEC Regent motor buses with similar bodies were ordered at the same time. The trolleybuses were numbered 1-44 (FUF 1-44), and the first was delivered in March 1939. The Corporation trams had been painted in cream and burgundy, but a stipulation of the 1938 Act was that Corporation and Company buses should share a common livery and destination-screen layout. The trolleybuses were therefore painted in BH&D's red with cream roof and window surrounds and were fitted with that company's London-style destination screen boxes, inherited from Thomas Tilling. 'Brighton Hove & District Transport' was the fleetname carried by both operators, beneath which the Corporation vehicles carried the town's coat of arms.

The Weymann bodywork was particularly handsome, with a gently curving frontal profile, unbroken save for a slightly protruding destination box. Of five-bay construction, it featured metal louvres over the windows that tapered at the corners and added to the curvaceous appearance, while a novel idea was the fitting of rubber mudguards to minimise damage. The trolleybuses were fitted with 80hp Crompton Parkinson motors, and electrical equipment was by Allen West, whose factory was a few hundred yards from the Corpora-

tion's depot in Lewes Road. Because of Brighton's hilly terrain they were fitted with 'coasting' and 'run-back' brakes.

Boarding one of the Brighton trolleys was a bit like entering an Odeon cinema. The ceilings were covered in Alhambrinal, a textured, beige-coloured material that was divided into panels separated by polished wooden beading. Each panel was lined out in black, and those in the centre of the ceiling had a green and gold motif at each corner. These ceilings were highly praised but were never liked by the writer

Right: The dawn of a new era. With registration plates still to be affixed, Brighton Corporation AEC trolleybus No 1 (FUF 1) stands outside the Weymann factory at Addlestone in 1939. Note the chrome handle area on the driver's door still lacking a handle; also the smart chrome hubcaps, which would later succumb to red paint. *Metro-Cammell-Weymann / Eric Surfleet collection*

Right: Another official view, this time featuring No 3 and showing to good advantage the graceful lines of the Weymann body design. Already the name of Winston Robinson, General Manager of Brighton Corporation's Transport Department, has been applied aft of the front nearside wheel. Note also the single fog lamp fitted on the nearside — a short-lived feature. *Metro-Cammell-Weymann / Eric Surfleet collection*

Above: An important safety consideration in the operation of trolleybuses is the adequate insulation of electrical components. Here No 24 is being sprayed with water to check for any leakage of current to the bodywork via the chassis. *Metro-Cammell-Weymann / Malcolm Keeping collection*

(GK-J), in whose opinion they gave the saloons a dismal, gloomy appearance, especially after dark and particularly upstairs, where the Alhambrinal became liberally coated with nicotine from generations of cigarette smokers.

Presumably for the sake of standardisation the front bulkhead was the same as that on the motor buses and was therefore unnecessarily high. The area below the bulkhead windows was finished in black corded rubber, in the centre of which was a small white plastic plate bearing the legend 'Bus No. xx' — a feature that would be perpetuated through to the 'Sixties and the forward-entrance Leyland PD2s. The bulkhead window on the driver's side was fitted with a sliding section enabling him to speak with the conductor. Seats were covered in a green and beige moquette and had dark-green backs.

The window frames were of dark polished wood, and above the front lower-deck windows was mounted a double display case in the same polished wood, in which were displayed four advertisements. At least one of these was usually for a local cinema, the display case allowing them to be replaced once or twice a week when there was a change of programme.

Always keen to make a few pounds from advertising, the Corporation posted a small advertisement between the bulkhead

Right: Another important check to be made before a vehicle is released to the operator is the tilt test, seen here being undertaken at the Weymann factory. The gauge on the bodywork on Brighton No 1 indicates a tilt of 32°, but note that the gauge on the ramp shows only 25°, the difference being explained by the play in the vehicle's suspension. *Metro-Cammell-Weymann / Malcolm Keeping collection*

Above: The *Evening Argus* was on hand to record the delivery of No 1 to the depot in Lewes Road in the spring of 1939. The drawbar is still attached, and the gentleman looks inquisitively down at it as he puffs on his cigarette. *Evening Argus / Malcolm Keeping collection*

windows and another on the panel below, although it has to be said that posters were never fixed to the Alhambrinal-covered cove panels. External advertising was exploited to the full, positions being carried over from tramway days. Curved 'wrap-around' adverts were applied to the front and rear corners between decks, as well as the usual side panels. On the lower deck the offside rear corner was used, as well as the usual 'lower rear' position below the rear window, whilst a double-crown-size advert was carried behind the offside rear wheel. The rear waistband position above the rear platform window could not be used, due to the positioning of the numberplate and rear light, but even so the trolleys sported a creditable nine external adverts (although this was to be overshadowed by the motor buses, some of which managed to display no fewer than seventeen!).

The timing of the final changeover from trams to trolleybuses could hardly have been worse. The last tram ran into the depot on 31 August 1939, the trolleybuses taking over the following day. Two days later the country was at war.

Left: 'The Old Order Changeth', announced the *Brighton & Hove Herald* 8 April 1939. Accompanying its article was this photograph of No 1 on test at the Old Steine. Note on the rear platform the employee giving the 'thumbs up', suggesting that all was going well. *Brighton & Hove Herald / Malcolm Keeping collection*

Brand-new trolleybuses in the smart red and cream livery agreed under the Transport Agreement were given grey roofs — or, in the case of Nos 1–8, painted in all-over khaki — to make them less conspicuous from the air. The all-khaki 'buses were so treated because, fearing that a bomb landing on Lewes Road depot could destroy the entire fleet, the Corporation parked a number of trolleybuses overnight at The Level, where they were shielded from the air by the surrounding trees (hence the khaki livery).

To keep its side of the bargain Brighton, Hove & District ordered eight trolleybuses — a first for a Tilling Group company. The vehicles were broadly similar to the Corporation's, being AEC 661Ts with 54-seat Weymann bodies. They were numbered consecutively in the BH&D fleet as 6340-7 and arrived with matching registrations BPN 340-7. However, as their entry into service was delayed until after the war these registrations were surrendered, and they eventually received a 'mish-mash' of numbers in the 'CPM' series, viz 61, 62, 53, 375, 101, 102, 521 and 997.

Following the cessation of hostilities the Corporation trolleybuses regained their original livery and were joined in service by the eight Brighton, Hove & District AECs, which had been stored throughout the war at the company's Whitehawk garage in Arundel Road, close to the seafront at Black Rock. When the war finished it was found that their motors had been badly affected by the salty air, and some remedial treatment was required before they could enter service.

It is frequently said that the BH&D trolleybuses were virtually identical to the Corporation vehicles, aside from lacking the Brighton coat of arms, but there were in fact numerous differences by which the trained eye could identify the two operators' trolleys. Probably the most obvious, at least in the eyes of the writer, were the fewer advertisement spaces, only four being carried on Company vehicles — double-deck sides, target (offside rear corner) and lower rear. This could, of course, be deceptive when one saw a Corporation 'bus without a full set of adverts (not that that was a very common occurrence), but not to worry! There were other identification points. The destination boxes on the BH&D trolleys were flush-fitting, and the rear light was fitted at lower-deck waist level, beside the 'stopping' sign rather than the number-plate. When new the BH&D trolleybuses had fixed nearside windscreens, but opening windscreens were fitted at a fairly early stage. Company vehicles had small gold (later black) fleet numbers instead of the Corporation's large ornate gold numerals, and, in later years at least, they sported black (rather than red) wheels, as was also the case with the motor-bus fleet.

Above: Engaged on driver-training duties in the early spring of 1939 (note the bare trees), No 1 passes the Royal Pavilion on its way to the Old Steine. This would have been a hectic time for the Corporation's Transport Department as sufficient drivers were trained for the changeover. The task was completed by September — a credit to the staff at Lewes Road depot. *Malcolm Keeping collection*

Internally the differences were many and immediately obvious. Ceilings were painted in brilliant white and lacked the wooden beading, giving a much more light and airy appearance. The display cabinets were not fitted, although they did carry advertisement frames beneath the bulkhead windows, posters above these windows being fixed directly to the paintwork. Between the bulkhead windows was a three-sided frame into which could be slipped a card; if memory serves correctly this was usually for the Imperial (later Essoldo) Cinema.

In 1948 a further 11 trolleybuses were ordered — three for BH&D and eight for the Corporation. This time the chassis chosen was the BUT 9611T, British United Traction being the marketing name used postwar for trolleybuses produced by AEC and Leyland. They were much more powerful than their prewar counterparts, having 120hp motors. Weymann 56-seat bodywork was fitted to the three BH&D vehicles, numbered 6391-3 (DNJ 991-3), and to six of the Corporation 'buses, Nos 45–50 (HUF 45-50).

A year earlier Brighton Corporation had purchased some AEC Regent III motor buses with particularly handsome Weymann bodies of four-bay construction. The trolleybuses, however, retained their five-bay layout and were, in reality, barely different from their prewar counterparts. All had flush-fitting destination screens, and the half-drop windows were of the winding type rather than the 'pinch and

Above: Brand-new Weymann-bodied AEC No 5 stands proudly by the entrance to the Corporation's Lewes Road depot. On the right of the picture a tram awaits its fate, while to the left is the fan of tram tracks, which would be replaced by a simple set of wires with a turning-circle at the far end of the garage. Note the massive coils of wiring against the far wall. *The Omnibus Society*

Above: Time for celebration, with the official launch of Brighton's trolleybuses on 1 June 1939. Suitably bedecked with flags, No 1 leads No 9 at the Old Steine. The crowds have gathered to see the switch (located on the platform of No 1) flicked, energising the system, as an inspector on the platform of following No 9 looks on anxiously to ensure that all goes to plan. Note that already it has been found necessary to apply a 'To & From PALACE PIER' transfer above the rear wheel. In the background can be seen contrasting forms of transport in the form of an equally new AEC Regent, on the former tram route to Dyke Road, and surviving trams bound for Elm Grove. *Evening Argus / Malcolm Keeping collection*

Left: With the Royal Pavilion as a backdrop Corporation No 1 glides by with guests aboard for the inaugural trip on 1 June 1939. The tram traction pole by the parking sign has been rendered redundant by new poles necessitated by the heavier trolleybus wiring. *Evening Argus / Malcolm Keeping collection*

squeeze' spring-loaded variety. The feature that made them stand out, however, was a quite minor one: in place of the inward-opening windows fitted to the front upper-deck windows of the AECs the BUTs had opening ventilators not unlike those fitted to utility double-deckers, the lower edge being quite thick and painted cream. It was quite amazing what a difference this made to the vehicles' overall appearance. Two of the Corporation's eight BUTs were delivered in chassis form and were stored at Lewes Road until 1950, when they were sent to Weymann for bodying. They emerged as Nos 51/2 (LCD 51/2) and were virtually identical to the 1948 batch; the only difference that comes to mind was the fitting of leather straps for standing passengers in the lower saloon.

Right: In a scene recalling a famous Southern Railway advertisement a child gazes in awe at a newly delivered trolleybus as an inspector points to the overhead. The photograph would have been taken *circa* June 1939 outside the depot in Lewes Road, with Preston Barracks (nowadays the site of a retail park) on the right. In the background is the railway viaduct carrying the Kemp Town branch, by this time already closed to passenger traffic. *Evening Argus / Malcolm Keeping collection*

Right: Heralding a new beginning for public transport in Brighton, No 3 (FUF 3), one of the initial 44-strong fleet of Weymann-bodied AEC trolleybuses delivered to Brighton Corporation, stands in the Old Steine when new in 1939. Whilst this was (and remains) a popular location for photographers there are few colour views of Brighton's trolleybuses with immaculate chrome front wheels and fog lamps and without advertisements around the front corners of the bodywork. *Leeds Transport Historical Society, courtesy Online Transport Archive*

Left: AECs Nos 26 and 20 stand in the sunshine at the Old Steine. All appears tranquil, and it is difficult to believe that war has broken out — a situation confirmed by the masking of the nearside headlights and the application of white paint to the tips of the front wings. Scrutiny of the road in the foreground reveals where the tram tracks have been removed. *John Bishop collection*

Left: Contrasting with the previous picture is this photograph of No 5 looking drab in its wartime khaki livery despite being still relatively new. The lack of people is eerie given the sunshine, although the coastal area was a restricted area; this would surely have affected the movement of the populace and traditional British habits by the seaside which had to be put on hold. *W. J. Haynes / Southdown Enthusiasts' Club*

Left: BH&D ordered eight AECs, to be registered BPN 340-7, matching their Tilling-inspired fleet numbers (6340-7). No 6345 (BPN 345) is depicted in this official view of the rear offside and the destination screen is seen to be mounted flush with the bodywork. The registration numbers were never taken up and new numbers were allocated, the trolleybuses being stored throughout the war. *Metro-Cammell-Weymann / Eric Surfleet*

Above: Pictured at the Old Steine on 20 April 1948, BH&D 6347 (CPM 997) shows off the flush-mounted destination screen that distinguished it from the Corporation trolleybuses. It is difficult to believe that, although nearly eight years old, the vehicle had been in service for only two years when the photograph was taken. *Alan B. Cross*

Right: The postwar Weymann body on a BUT chassis was a most handsome design, as demonstrated at the Old Steine by Brighton, Hove & District No 6393 of 1948. A side-by-side comparison with Corporation No 26 reveals the detail differences between prewar and postwar examples. *Alan B. Cross*

Left: An official photograph showing the cab of a Brighton Corporation BUT trolleybus, possibly No 50. Visible are the mains switches (on the ceiling), the contactor gear (alongside the driver's seat) and the brake, accelerator and handbrake in the foreground.
Metro-Cammell-Weymann / Malcolm Keeping collection

Left: Colour photographs taken before 1960 are few and far between, so this mid-1950s view of postwar Weymann-bodied BUT No 45 approaching the Old Steine terminus of route 48 from Lewes Road Barracks is particularly noteworthy. Numerically the first of the postwar batch delivered in 1947, No 45 would see 12 years' service before being sold for further service in Bournemouth, thus staying by the seaside!
Michael Dryhurst

Right: An official view of No 52, numerically the last trolleybus for Brighton Corporation — and how smart it looks! The chassis was delivered in 1948 and stored, not being bodied until 1951; the photograph is dated 20 September 1951. *Metro-Cammell-Weymann / Malcolm Keeping collection*

Right: No publication on Brighton's trolleybuses would be complete without a look at the interior of one of the Corporation's vehicles — BUT/Weymann No 50 — complete with ornate Alhambrinal ceiling. This is the view rearwards on the upper deck. *Metro-Cammell-Weymann / Malcolm Keeping collection*

Right: A lower-deck interior view of No 50, showing the moquette design and the beautiful detailing on the ceiling. *Metro-Cammell-Weymann / Malcolm Keeping collection*

3. The Routes

The tram routes had, in most cases, radiated outwards from Old Steine and the replacing trolleybus routes tended to do the same, although there were exceptions.

The Old Steine terminus was, for some reason, always known by the Corporation as 'Aquarium', although it was some distance from that establishment. Destination blinds showed 'AQUARIUM OLD STEINE'.

The Dyke Road tram route (N) was the only one not to be replaced by trolleybuses, services 51 (via London Road and Preston Circus) and 52 (via Sea Front, West Street and Brighton Station) being worked by motor buses.

Tram routes B and D (Beaconsfield Villas/Ditchling Road–Fiveways) in effect formed a circular service, as a tram arriving at Fiveways on route B continued as a D, returning to the Aquarium via Beaconsfield Villas. They were replaced directly by trolleybus routes 26A (via Ditchling Road) and 46A (via Beaconsfield Villas). These two routes effectively became short workings of new routes 26 and 46; wiring had been erected northwards from Fiveways along Ditchling Road to its junction with Surrenden Road, and both the 26 and 46 were extended from Fiveways to cover the new section. In 1948 both services were extended further north to a new turning-circle in Larkfield Way. Then, in 1951, the 26 was extended via Carden Hill to a new terminus at Hollingbury; the 46 was diverted at the top of Beaconsfield Villas to run via Surrenden Road, Braybon Avenue and Carden Avenue to the same terminus at Hollingbury. Trolleys running to Hollingbury on service 46 returned to the Old Steine on service 26 and *vice versa*.

The Lewes Road tram route (L) became trolleybus route 48 and was the first to be converted, the wiring on this route giving access to Lewes Road depot.

The Queen's Park Road service (Q) was extended via Rock Gardens and St James's Street to Old Steine and became circular service 41, trolleybuses usually showing 'CIRCULAR via St James's St' as the ultimate destination. 'Cross-country' route C from Seven Dials to Rock Gardens via New England Road, Union Road, Elm Grove and Queen's Park Road was similarly extended via St James's Street to Old Steine, then continuing via North Road and Brighton Station to its starting-point at Seven Dials, creating a second circular service numbered 42; these 'buses showed 'CIRCULAR via Brighton Stn'. Both St James's Street and North Road have long since been made one-way and it now seems hard to believe that trolleybuses once traversed these narrow thoroughfares

Above: A rare photograph dating from August 1939, mere days before the trams disappeared from the streets of Brighton. Weymann-bodied AEC Regent 63 makes its way down Queen's Park Road working tram route Q; although the blind shows route 41, the destination is shown as Rock Gardens, and the 'via' screen has not been fully wound up so as not to reveal 'ST JAMES'S STREET'. Note that the trolleybus wires are already up, the trams using only the positive wire; also the fact that trams were restricted to a single track at this point near Albion Hill. Following withdrawal in February 1965 No 63 would pass into preservation and regularly attends rallies to this day.
Ronald Keeping

Above: The storm clouds are gathering for World War 2 and time is running out for Class E tram No 71, photographed in Queen's Park Road, with the main headlight already masked. The tram overhead has been taken down, and the trolleybus overhead strung up in its place in order that the trams can continue until the changeover on 1 September 1939. The view also reveals that the traction poles have been replaced, save one surviving temporarily with white-painted section to show where the point is located for the single-to double-track working. *Ronald Keeping*

Above: There always seemed to be some confusion as to the ultimate destination of route 48, variously described as Barracks, Coombe Road or plain old Lewes Road! Corporation postwar Weymann-bodied BUT No 48 is seen in London Road just about to diverge at St Peter's Church for Lewes Road. *Eric Surfleet*

in both directions; indeed, St James's Street was particularly hazardous, and trolleybus drivers had to take extra care not to hit shop blinds stretching across the pavement. Clockwise 41s and 42s leaving the bottom of St James's Street originally crossed directly over Old Steine past the War Memorial to Electric House, on the corner of Castle Square; later they were diverted to run south to the Aquarium terminus, and the wiring across the centre of Old Steine was removed.

Tram route E (Old Steine–Race Hill) was replaced directly by trolleybus 43A, whilst BH&D route 44 ran from Seven Dials to Race Hill, replacing the whole of tram route C. The 44 service was the only trolleybus service to be operated solely by BH&D, but on its inception in 1939, due to the storage of the Company trolleybuses, it was of necessity worked by Corporation vehicles. Following the outbreak of war certain services had been curtailed, and the Corporation therefore had sufficient spare trolleybuses to cover for the Company vehicles. From 1946 the 44 was extended via Manor Hill to Black Rock, allowing BH&D trolleybuses to operate from their 'own' garage in Arundel Road. Service 43A was also extended over the same route, Black Rock journeys being numbered 43, but this was a summer-only extension. The turning 'loop' at Black Rock was the only point where Brighton trolleybuses actually ran along the seafront.

The 44 was interesting in that it crossed over Brighton Racecourse at the top of Manor Hill. On race days this section of road would be closed, and trolleybuses from Seven Dials would terminate at the top of Freshfield Road, turning under battery power. One trolleybus would operate a shuttle service from the other side of the racecourse to Black Rock.

Two other trolleybus routes introduced in June and July 1939 proved short-lived: circular services 40 (Aquarium–London Road–Seven Dials–Brighton Station–Aquarium) and 40A (Aquarium–London Road–Seven Dials) were withdrawn in September 1939, being replaced by service 42. Introduced at the same time was the 40B, an occasional peak-hour only service running from Brighton station to the Aquarium via North Road. This lasted until 1955, but its operation was very infrequent, being confined mainly to summer Saturdays and Sundays when huge numbers of day-trippers needed to be carried from the station to the seafront and *vice versa*.

This, then, was the core of Brighton's trolleybus network, introduced in 1939 and destined to remain largely unchanged for almost 20 years, until the first stage of abandonment in March 1959.

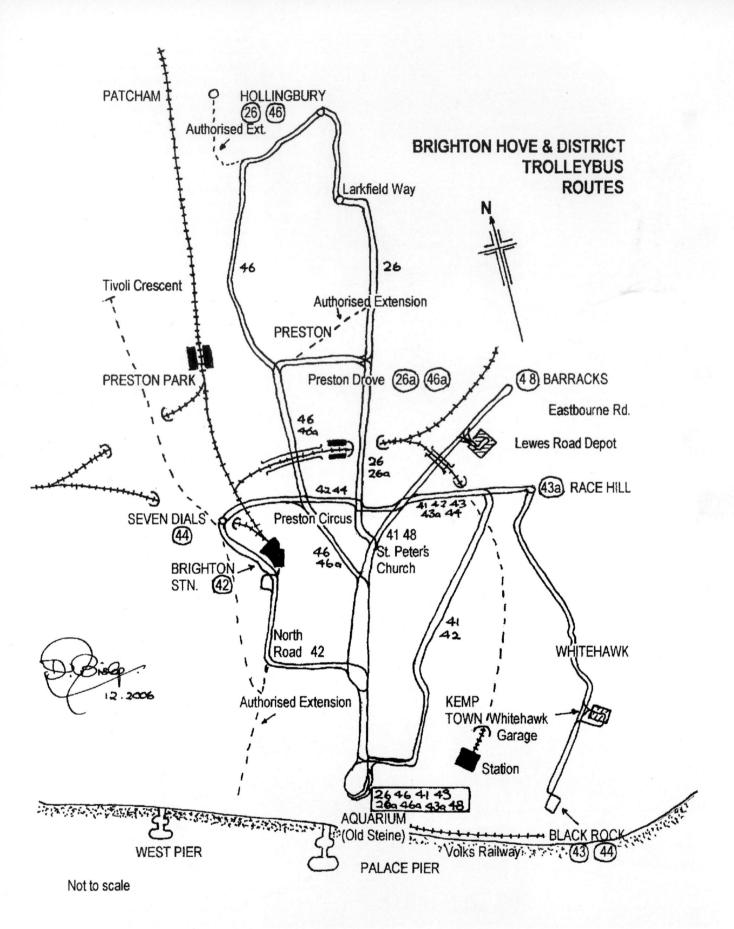

PATCHAM

HOLLINGBURY
26 46
Authorised Ext.

BRIGHTON HOVE & DISTRICT
TROLLEYBUS
ROUTES

N

Larkfield Way

46   26

Tivoli Crescent

Authorised Extension

PRESTON

PRESTON PARK

Preston Drove 26a 46a

4 8 BARRACKS

Eastbourne Rd.

46
46a

Lewes Road Depot

26
26a

42 44

43a RACE HILL

41 42 43
43a 44

SEVEN DIALS
44

Preston Circus

41 48
St. Peter's
Church

46
46a

BRIGHTON
STN. 42

North
Road 42

41
42

WHITEHAWK

D. Bishop
12.2006

Authorised Extension

KEMP
TOWN Whitehawk
Garage

Station

26 46 41 43
26a 46a 43a 48

BLACK ROCK

WEST PIER

AQUARIUM
(Old Steine)

Volks Railway 43 44

PALACE PIER

Not to scale

BRIGHTON HOVE & DISTRICT
— TRANSPORT —

OFFICIAL

TIME TABLE

AND MAP OF ROUTES

3D.

SUMMER 1948

BRIGHTON HOVE & DISTRICT
— TRANSPORT —

Official Opening Ceremony of the Corporation Transport Undertaking ... take place at 12 noon on Thursday, 1st June, 1939. In the afternoon, ... th part of the re-organisation scheme will take place, in this case on ... ling and Beaconsfield Roads, when the existing tram services will ... own and replaced by new and revised services operated by trolley ... anges will also be made on certain bus routes in this area, and ... full details of the re-organisation are given below:

NEW ROUTES

... uses).—AQUARIUM (Old Steine) AND SURRENDEN ROAD, ...
... ns, St. Peter's Church and Ditching Road.
... e for Surrenden Road and Ditching Road.
... Road for Aquarium at 19, 39, and 59 minutes past each hour.

... ROAD | WEEKDAYS | | SUNDAYS
... ARIUM | First Bus | Last Bus | First Bus | Last Bus
7.20	11.20		11.20
7.39	11.19		11.19
then 11.34		9.39	then 11.34

... QUARIUM (Old Steine) AND SURRENDEN ROAD,
... on Road, Preston Circus, Beaconsfield Villas,
... ad.

... Road at 10, 30, and 50 minutes past each hour.
... quarium at 7, 27, and 47 minutes past each hour.

... | WEEKDAYS | | SUNDAYS
... | First Bus | Last Bus | First Bus | Last Bus
| 7.12 | 11.10 | 9.10 | 11.10 |
| then 7.27 | 11.27 | 9.27 | 11.27 |

...SED ROUTES

... (Old Steine), AQUARIUM (Old Steine), DITCHLING ROAD,
... with Route No. 26).—This route replaces the former tram Route "D."
46a (Trolley Buses).—AQUARIUM (Old Steine), DITCHLING ROAD,
BEACONSFIELD VILLAS, PRESTON CIRCUS,
AQUARIUM (Old Steine).—This route replaces the former tram Route "B."
Together with Route No. 46, a 5-minute service is given over Ditchling Road.

AQUARIUM (Old Steine), PRESTON DROVE, DITCHLING ROAD,
... with Route No. 46, a 5-minute service is given over Beaconsfield
... Villas.

No. 8 (Motor Buses).—DYKE ROAD AND PRESTON DROVE (Hollingbury).
This route will terminate at LODER ROAD (Junction with Surrenden Road).
Times will remain unaltered over the remaining portions of the route except
that the last journeys leaving Loder Road will be at 11.1 p.m., 11.11 p.m.
(8a), 11.21 p.m., 11.31 p.m. (8a) (five minutes earlier than existing times).

No. 8a (Motor Buses).—DYKE ROAD AND HOLLINGBURY (Surrenden
Road) will terminate at PEACOCK LANE (Junction with Surrenden
Road). Times will remain unaltered over the remaining portions of the route
except that the last journeys leaving Peacock Lane 2 minutes later than
existing times from Hollingbury (buses leaving Peacock Lane will be at 11.8 p.m. and
11.28 p.m. (five minutes earlier than existing times).

THIS CANCELS PREVIOUS ANNOUNCEMENT

The Brighton Hove and District Omnibus Co., Ltd., Conway Street, Hove, 3. Issued by The Brighton Corporation Transport Dept., Lewes Road, Brighton. Tel.: Brighton 6141
Tel.: Hove 1002-3.
30/5/39.

Route 48: Old Steine–Preston Barracks

Left: Route 48 never expanded further than the tram route serving Preston Barracks and Lewes Road depot. Just a few yards to the south is Coombe Road, where powers were granted for an extension but never taken up. Postwar Corporation Weymann-bodied BUT No 45 waits to leave with a light load for the Aquarium (in reality Old Steine). The advertisement represents something of a conflict of interest outside Schweppes! *W. J. Haynes / Southdown Enthusiasts' Club*

Right: Pictured outside Apex Motorcycles — a favourite location for the photographer — Weymann-bodied BUT No 48 has almost reached the Aquarium (Old Steine) terminus of route 48. In the 1950s a win of £200,000 from an investment of two old pennies certainly represented pennies from Heaven! *Eric Surfleet*

Left: Heading north along the Lewes Road, with St Peter's Church in the background, Corporation AEC No 33 looks its age in this late-1950s view. The route was converted to motor-bus operation in 1959, but trolleybuses continued to use the wiring for depot workings. Note the complete absence of other road traffic, aside from an early-1950s Austin 25cwt florist's van. *Eric Surfleet*

Right: Pictured just south of St Peter's Church, 1951-built Corporation BUT/Weymann No 51 leaves the London Road to head up the Lewes Road during the mid-1950s. This was a time when Northampton Shoe Repairers was a household name in Brighton. *Eric Surfleet*

Left: Corporation No 14 was an early casualty, being withdrawn in 1958, but is seen here at the Old Steine in happier times. Behind is a prewar AEC Regent on route 40B to Brighton station, which operated only at weekends during the summer and until 1955 was normally worked by trolleybuses. *Photobus*

Right: As a seaside resort Brighton is synonymous with holidaymakers and candyfloss, which nearly ruined this view of postwar BUT No 46 in the Old Steine. In the background is a prewar AEC Regent waiting to depart for Dyke Road. *D. A. Jones / London Trolleybus Preservation Society*

Above: Trolleybuses running anti-clockwise on Queen's Park circular routes 41 and 42 stopped in the Old Steine outside J. Lyons on the corner of St James's Street. Here AEC/Weymann No 14 stands proudly in the sunshine as it collects passengers before heading up St James's Street. A study of the advertisements makes for fascinating reading: Brobat cleaning fluid cost one shilling (5p) a bottle — and 'why not visit the Brighton Zoo', although the latter, at Withdean Stadium, could be reached not by trolleybus but by BH&D motor-bus routes 5 and 15. *W. J. Haynes / Southdown Enthusiasts' Club*

Below: A delightful view of a Brighton Corporation 1948 Weymann-bodied BUT at the Old Steine by the junction of St James's Street. Seen when almost new, No 47 had not yet gained its wrap-round advertisements. Route 41 was a shortened version of the route 42, omitting Brighton station but still serving the Queen's Park Road area. *W. J. Haynes / Southdown Enthusiasts' Club*

Opposite top: Trolleybuses running clockwise on the 41 route would leave the Old Steine on the outer wiring, which became redundant upon the conversion of routes 41, 42 and 48 to motor bus. This photograph was taken in March 1959. *John Bishop / Online Transport Archive*

Opposite bottom: Heading towards the Old Steine whilst running clockwise on route 41, Corporation AEC No 29 negotiates the turn from Rock Gardens into St James's Street. Note the United public house building on the corner and the tiled face promoting ales and stouts. This location has changed very little in the half century since the photograph was taken in the summer of 1955. *Malcolm Keeping*

Above: It is quite unusual to find photographs taken at the junction of Rock Gardens and St James's Street, especially of this quality. This location was the terminus of tram route Q, so now Brighton Corporation AEC No 22 would have been on new territory in 1939. Passengers have gathered at the bus stop in Rock Gardens, possibly waiting for an anti-clockwise 41 or 42 trolleybus. *W. J. Haynes / Southdown Enthusiasts' Club*

Left: Trolleybus route 42 basically took over from the station tram route and the short-lived 40 group of services, although the 40B continued on specials and at peak times. This view, recorded at Brighton station in the 1950s, features Corporation AEC trolleybus No 37 and AEC Regent III motor bus 88 as the crews catch up on gossip. *D. A. Jones / London Trolleybus Preservation Society*

Above: Having left Brighton station on a clockwise working, Corporation AEC No 6 enounters an AEC Regent at Seven Dials; from here it will descend to Preston Circus, *en route* passing beneath the railway bridges in New England Road. It will be noted from the overhead that there was a facility for trolleybuses to turn back to the station, although this was rarely if ever used once the 41 and 42 had taken over from the 40-group routes. Authorisation was granted for trolleybuses to run up Dyke Road, but the Corporation never took up the option. *Glyn Kraemer-Johnson collection*

Above: A scene from early 1959, shortly before the 42 was converted to motor-bus operation using the Corporation's new Leyland PD2s such as No 51. Having passed though the feed wires strung across the junction, BH&D AEC/Weymann trolleybus No 340 approaches the Old Steine. Note the Southdown Northern Counties-bodied Guy Arab (511) on local route 13. *Glyn Kraemer-Johnson collection*

Route 44: Seven Dials–Black Rock

Left: BH&D Weymann-bodied AEC No 6344 turns to the right towards the southern end of the racecourse and Black Rock on cross-country route 44. At this stage it has not quite reached the frog allowing exit from the turning circle at Race Hill. Compared with the Corporation vehicles this looks more elegant without the wrap-round advertisements. In the background note the dark blue County Borough of Brighton Dennis. *W. J. Haynes / Southdown Enthusiasts' Club*

Right: Brighton, Hove & District Weymann-bodied BUT 6391 has reached the top of Manor Hill from Whitehawk on route 44 to Seven Dials, the one route which did not go via Old Steine. The fenced-off section to the left is part of the racecourse. Note in the background all the work in progress above Whitehawk for the continued development of eastern Brighton in the postwar years. In this scene, one pole and bracket arm supports both sets of wires. *W. J. Haynes / Southdown Enthusiasts' Club*

Left: Company BUT 391 had been renumbered from 6391 by the time this view was taken as it turns onto the seafront road before laying over at Black Rock on the long route 44. Looking inland, the scene has changed very little here over the years, but seaward the transformation has been dramatic with the development — still ongoing — of Brighton Marina. *Glyn Kraemer-Johnson collection*

Right: Brighton, Hove & District purchased only three trolleybuses postwar, these being Weymann-bodied BUTs Nos 6391-3. No 392, as latterly renumbered, is seen in Arundel Road having just passed the frog for exiting trolleybuses from the depot on the extreme right. Within a few minutes it will be at Black Rock. Note the diminutive Austin Seven in the background along with the small business shops of the day.
Glyn Kraemer-Johnson collection

Right: Route 44 (Seven Dials–Black Rock) was normally the preserve of Brighton, Hove & District AEC and BUT vehicles, although the Corporation was responsible for the overhead. Here BH&D AEC No 344, renumbered in 1956 when the company dropped the leading '6' from its fleet numbers, descends the steep Manor Hill on its way to Black Rock, with the Race Hill in the background.
Michael Dryhurst

Left: On a murky day in the late 1950s BH&D No 391 (formerly 6391) stands at the Black Rock terminus of route 44 — the only point at which trolleybuses actually reached the seafront. This area has since changed dramatically with the building and development of Brighton Marina.
Michael Dryhurst

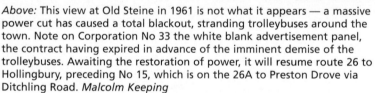

Above: This view at Old Steine in 1961 is not what it appears — a massive power cut has caused a total blackout, stranding trolleybuses around the town. Note on Corporation No 33 the white blank advertisement panel, the contract having expired in advance of the imminent demise of the trolleybuses. Awaiting the restoration of power, it will resume route 26 to Hollingbury, preceding No 15, which is on the 26A to Preston Drove via Ditchling Road. *Malcolm Keeping*

Above: Brighton Corporation No 23 provides a night-time study of the fine lines of the Weymann body while standing at the Old Steine waiting to depart for Hollingbury on route 26. Just visible is a bus substitution for a trolleybus in the 46 lane. The neon lights belong to a Fortes restaurant — now a Harry Ramsden fish-and-chip emporium. *John Bishop / Online Transport Archive*

Left: At Old Steine (Aquarium) can be seen Brighton Corporation BUT No 52 — in the eyes of the authors, the last word in trolleybus design. She waits ready to depart for Hollingbury on route 26; the climb up Ditchling Road will be effortless and, more importantly, clean with no exhaust fumes. Visible in the background is the Brighton Corporation Information Office. *John Bishop collection*

Above: In this strikingly animated view Brighton Corporation No 40, a prewar AEC, ploughs through the rainwater in 1961 with misted windows at the start of its journey from Hollingbury to the Aquarium. It will have arrived here from Carden Avenue on the left on route 46 prior to continuing as a 26. Note the classic Morris J in the background and the well-known local bakery advertised on the front nearside. The prominent family-planning advert adorned some of the trolleybuses only in their final months. *Glyn Kraemer-Johnson collection*

Above: Hollingbury terminus in 1961, with Nos 36 and 29 waiting to depart on routes 26 and 46 respectively. The crews chat before hopping aboard for their 20-minute runs back to the Aquarium. Note the unique Brighton-type bus shelters, very necessary this close to the breezy South Downs, especially in the winter. *Malcolm Keeping*

Route 26A: Old Steine–Preston Drove via Ditchling Road

Above: This undated view of No 1 under the frog where the St James's Street routes 41 and 42 met shows it on layover prior to taking up service on route 26A. Whilst the trolleybus looks well cared for one could not say the same for AEC Regent No 61 behind. *Photobus*

Left: It is early spring 1961 at the Old Steine, and soon Brighton Corporation No 17 will be on its way to Preston Drove via Ditchling Road. At journey's end the screen will be changed to route 46A for the return journey via Beaconsfield Road, completing the circular run. *John Bishop / Online Transport Archive*

Left: Part-torn final destination screen and part wound-up screen for the 'via' section hardly created a good impression in the final weeks of trolleybus operation by Brighton Corporation in 1961 as seen in this flash view of No 6 at Old Steine. There are plenty of trolleybuses in the background, whilst to the far right an almost-new Bristol Lodekka in cream looms out of the darkness.
John Bishop / Online Transport Archive

Above: This superb view recorded on 4 September 1960 features Corporation No 20 at the top of Beaconsfield Road and turning into Preston Drove for the short run to Ditchling Road. This would be the furthest extent north for the 26A and 46A and replaced the trams over the northernmost point of the original tram network. *A. D. Packer*

Above: Few photographs exist of Brighton Corporation **vehicles** inside Lewes Road depot because it was very much forbidden territory, but in May 1961 access was granted for this lovely view **of 1939**-built Weymann-bodied AEC No 38, heading a line of four similar vehicles under the 'out road' wiring. Vehicles would enter on the **right** wiring, turning in the far background without the need to de-pole. Just visible to the left is numerically the Corporation's **first** Leyland PD2, No 51 (WCD 51), one of an initial batch of 20 delivered in 1959 for the first stage of trolleybus abandonment. *John Bishop / Online Transport Archive*

Left: The sylvan surroundings at the top of Braybon Avenue, with the South Downs in the background, form the setting for AEC No 43, inbound on route 46 on a gloriously sunny day in the late 1950s. Note that on this section of route bracket arms on one side of the road supported both sets of overhead wiring, making for a neat appearance. *Photobus*

Left: AEC No 23 waits to leave the Old Steine for Hollingbury on route 46, which, according to the 1957 timetable, would take a mere 22 minutes — a task impossible in today's traffic conditions. The photograph was taken on Whit Monday 22 May 1961, just weeks before such scenes were to pass into history. *John Bishop / Online Transport Archive*

Right: The graceful rear of the Weymann body design is shown to good effect in this view of 1939 AEC No 15 at rest in Carden Hill, Hollingbury, in May 1961. In the background are the South Downs. Note also the red granite-and-tarmac road surface used by the County Borough of Brighton. *John Bishop / Online Transport Archive*

Right: Weymann-bodied AEC No 4 stands at the bus stop in Larkfield Way, off Ditchling Road, before returning to the Old Steine in May 1961. Note the wiring for the turning-circle, installed in November 1948 when the 26 was extended from Surrenden Road, which had been used as a terminus for just four months before the final push to Hollingbury. The concrete bus shelter would last for more than 40 years from 1948 before being replaced by a modern structure. *John Bishop / Online Transport Archive*

Above: Returning to the town centre on route 46A from Hollingbury, Brighton Corporation AEC/Weymann No 27 of 1939 coasts down Beaconsfield Villas in May 1961. Although by this time maintenance was being kept to a minimum, its condition belies the fact that it would be withdrawn the following month upon closure of the Brighton system. *John Bishop / Online Transport Archive*

Left: Passing a copper beech that has just come into leaf, No 15 climbs Beaconsfield Road *en route* to Hollingbury in late May 1961. Just visible in the background (left) is the viaduct carrying the Brighton–Lewes railway line. Such a photograph would be impossible to replicate today, even with a motor bus, for this road is now one-way southbound, forming part of the A23 route into Brighton from the north.
John Bishop / Online Transport Archive

Right: A tranquil scene in Beaconsfield Villas in May 1961, with 1939-built AEC No 25 heading towards the Old Steine on route 46. Today these attractive houses have been converted into flats for the large student population attending the two universities in Brighton, and it is now literally a fight to find somewhere to park. *John Bishop / Online Transport Archive*

Left: The date is June 1961, and, with the advertising contract expired on the offside, the days are really numbered before No 25 is withdrawn after 22 years' valuable service. It is seen outside the 'Park View' public house, making the tight left turn from Surrenden Road into Preston Drove before turning right into Beaconsfield Villas on its way to the Old Steine on route 46. This location has changed very little, and one can still enjoy a pint in the sunshine and dream of days gone by when trolleybuses glided past! *John Bishop / Online Transport Archive*

Below: Still sporting a full set of advertisements, Weymann-bodied AEC No 41 stands at the bus stop on route 26. To the right is The Level, where one could relax or enjoy the large funfair or even the circus, when it came to town. In this view from June 1961 all is peaceful, but from the end of the month the area would echo to the roar of Brighton Corporation's new Leyland PD2s. *John Bishop / Online Transport Archive*

Left: In this shadowy view of AEC No 4 in May 1961 In Ditchling Road near the junction with Hollingdean Road, the trees are still struggling into full leaf, which affords us a sight of one of the wooden tram shelters that were a feature of Brighton for so many years.
John Bishop / Online Transport Archive

Left: At the junction of Ditchling Road and Preston Drove, better known as Fiveways, routes 26 and 26A diverged. In this view, recorded in May 1961, AEC No 33 of 1939 is seen making the turn from Ditchling Road into Preston Drove, from where it would return to the Old Steine as a 46A.
John Bishop / Online Transport Archive

Left: AEC/Weymann No 25 of 1939 passes the Larkfield Way turning-circle before continuing to Hollingbury in May 1961. With advertising contracts expiring some trolleybuses were adorned with short-term adverts, as here for 'Family Planning Services'. One can also see just how 'threadbare' the paintwork became as the shadows lengthened on the Brighton system. *John Bishop / Online Transport Archive*

Left: The hub of the Brighton trolleybus system was the Old Steine, which was virtually on the seafront. Pictured waiting in the 26 bay for Hollingbury, AEC/Weymann No 19, dating from 1939, would not last until the end, being withdrawn in November 1960, seven months before final closure of the system. Note (right) the tramway-era enquiry office, which was to remain in use long after the last trolleybus departed. *Photobus*

Right: Having arrived via Fiveways on route 26A, AEC/Weymann No 44, numerically Brighton's last prewar trolleybus, stands in Preston Drove, before turning left down Beaconsfield Road and returning to the Old Steine as a 46A. This part of Brighton has changed very little since the photograph was taken late in May 1961. *John Bishop / Online Transport Archive*

Left: Still looking the part after 22 years (albeit crying out for a lick of paint), AEC No 42 stands out well against the suburban housing of the Beaconsfield Villas / Preston Drove area in the latter days of trolleybus operation in May 1961. Bound for the Old Steine on route 26A, it demonstrates the practice of showing its ultimate destination as the Aquarium. *John Bishop / Online Transport Archive*

Left: All three Brighton, Hove & District BUT trolleybuses were sold to Bournemouth Corporation, where they were quite at home with the three-axle versions of the same type. Seen inside Bournemouth's Castle Lane depot is DNJ 992 (ex-BH&D 391) as delivered from Brighton in 1959. *Malcolm Keeping*

Left: With destination display rebuilt to its new operator's distinctive layout, ex-BH&D BUT/Weymann DNJ 994 looks right in full Bournemouth livery, complete with fleet number (294) applied in tramway style. *Malcolm Keeping*

Left: Another view of Bournemouth 294, formerly BH&D 392, this time at The Triangle, Bournemouth, on 19 June 1963. Along with the other two ex-BH&D BUTs it would serve its new owner until 1965. *Malcolm Keeping*

Above: In 1959 three of Brighton Corporation's BUT vehicles (Nos 45-7) were sold to Bournemouth, where they received that municipality's yellow livery and had their destination screens rebuilt. The quality of the work is apparent from this rear offside view of No 290 (HUF 47) at Bournemouth Corporation's Southcote Road depot in 1963. *John Bishop / Online Transport Archive*

Right: Brighton Corporation BUT No 47 dating from 1947 saw 12 years' service before being withdrawn in 1959 and sold on to Bournemouth Corporation, in whose employ it is seen here. Renumbered 290, it looked superb in Bournemouth's striking yellow livery. It is seen in 1962 in company with a fellow exile from Brighton; both vehicles are on layover, awaiting their next duties. *John Bishop / Online Transport Archive*

Right: Another view from 1963, featuring DNJ 992/4 (ex-BH&D Nos 390 and 392 respectively) inside their new home in Castle Lane, Bournemouth.
John Bishop / Online Transport Archive

Left: Corporation Nos 49 and 50 were sold to Bradford City Transport, which repainted them in its smart livery of blue and cream. With a different grille and having regained a fog lamp (a feature removed in Brighton), Bradford No 802 (HUF 49) is seen heading into the city in the early 1960s. *Malcolm Keeping*

Left: In its new guise as Bradford No 803, HUF 50 is seen on the city's pioneering trolleybus route of 1911. Despite its relative youth the vehicle was to have a brief life in its new home, being withdrawn in November 1962, albeit remaining in stock until 1965. *Malcolm Keeping*

Left: In 1959 Brighton Corporation Weymann-bodied BUT No 50 was sold to Bradford Corporation, becoming the latter's No 803. Bradford commenced trolleybus operation between Laisterdyke and Dudley Hill, and it is on this section the vehicle is seen in the early 1960s. *Malcolm Keeping*

Right: On 1 June 1963 suspected steering failure caused Bradford's HUF 49 to career into a traction pole and overturn. The aftermath of the accident was captured by the local newspaper. *Telegraph & Argus / Malcolm Keeping collection*

Right: Another view of the stricken 802, showing the sheared-off front axle and the transmission, as well as the support at the rear for the bamboo pole. Forward of the rear axle is the large electric motor which drove the trolleybus. *Telegraph & Argus / Malcolm Keeping collection*

Right: In this picture No 802 has been righted after its accident and is seen on suspended tow. Never repaired, it was to remain in store until 1965, when it was finally scrapped along with sister vehicle 803. *John Bishop / Online Transport Archive*

Left: With ready buyers for BUTs, Brighton Corporation's newest trolleybuses, Nos 51 and 52, were sold in 1959 along with the rest of the type, in this case to Maidstone, where they retained their existing fleet numbers. No 52 is seen outside Maidstone Corporation's Tonbridge Road depot soon after entering service in its new home town in the early 1960s. *Malcolm Keeping*

Left: Along with No 51, No 52 was to see service until the final day of Maidstone's trolleybuses in April 1967, by which time an oval grille had replaced the slatted original. Photographed just days before withdrawal, it was being pursued along Knightrider Street (home of Maidstone & District) by a Maidstone Corporation Leyland PD2 in the municipality's recently introduced livery of fiesta blue and cream. *John Bishop / Online Transport Archive*

Left: Following withdrawal by Maidstone Corporation No 52 passed into preservation and can today be found at the East Anglia Transport Museum at Carlton Colville, near Lowestoft, Suffolk. Although still in Maidstone livery it has regained its original front, and the interior has been carefully restored to its original Alhambrinal style. The only remaining Brighton Corporation trolleybus, it owes its condition both to the quality of its construction and to the dedication of the staff at Carlton Colville. *John Bishop / Online Transport Archive*

Above: Withdrawn along with the other BH&D trolleys after the first stage of trolleybus abandonment in 1959, No 340 passed into preservation as part of the British Transport Collection at Clapham in South London. When those premises closed it passed into the care of the London Transport Preservation Society, which showed it at the Historic Commercial Vehicle Club's Brighton rally in May 1967. This photograph, taken the following month, shows the vehicle at Conway Street, Hove, where it was being stored pending removal to its new home in Kent. *John Bishop / Online Transport Archive*

Below: In the spring of 1968 CPM 61 visited Middlesbrough, where on 31 March it participated in the inauguration of an extension to the Tees-side Railless Traction system. It was also used on a tour of the area, and is seen in surroundings totally alien to those experienced in Brighton. *John Bishop / Online Transport Archive*

Left: Little remains in Brighton to remind us of the halcyon days of the trolleybus. This view of Lewes Road depot shows the last traction pole to survive. Since this photograph was taken in May 2006 the right-hand gate has been replaced, resulting in the disappearance of the finial on the gate support. *John Bishop / Online Transport Archive*

Left: The location of this photograph, taken in May 2006, needs no introduction, but note that affixed to the wall between the two windows is an eye that once supported the overhead wiring. *John Bishop / Online Transport Archive*

Left: Close scrutiny of the railway viaduct in Beaconsfield Villas reveals an original tram rosette that subsequently supported the trolleybus wiring. The eyelet above supported the lighting, prompting the sobering thought that the rosette has remained there inert for more than 46 years. *John Bishop / Online Transport Archive*